FIVE GREAT NEEDS

by

Henry Clay Morrison

First Fruits Press
Wilmore, Kentucky
c2012

asburyseminary.edu
800.2ASBURY
204 North Lexington Avenue
Wilmore, Kentucky 40390

First Fruits
THE ACADEMIC OPEN PRESS OF ASBURY SEMINARY

ISBN: 9780984738717

Five Great Needs, by H.C. Morrison.
First Fruits Press, © 2012
Pentecostal Publishing Company, © 194-?

Digital version at http://place.asburyseminary.edu/firstfruitsheritagematerial/4/

Morrison, H. C. (Henry Clay), 1857-1942.
    Five great needs / by H.C. Morrison.
    Wilmore, Ky. : First Fruits Press, c2012.
    61 p. : 21 cm
    Reprint. Previously published: Previously published: Louisville, Ky. :
    Pentecostal Publishing Company, [194-?].
    ISBN: 9780984738762
    1. Christian life--Methodist authors. I. Title.
    BV4510 .M675 2012

Cover design by Haley Hill

asburyseminary.edu
800.2ASBURY
204 North Lexington Avenue
Wilmore, Kentucky 40390

First Fruits
THE ACADEMIC OPEN PRESS OF ASBURY SEMINARY

FIVE GREAT NEEDS

By

Rev. H. C. Morrison, D. D.

FIRST EDITION, JUNE 1
SECOND EDITION, JUNE 25
THIRD EDITION, JULY 19
FOURTH EDITION, AUGUST 27

PUBLISHED

By

PENTECOSTAL PUBLISHING COMPANY
LOUISVILLE, KENTUCKY

FOREWORD.

In my observation of conditions in our country, I have become fully persuaded that the Five Great Needs in order to the preservation of our homes, the spirituality of the Church, in its mission of evangelization of mankind, the building of character, enforcement of law, and the development of an intelligent, righteous and progressive civilization are:

First, good family government, with discipline and guidance, which produces obedience among children.

Second, the regeneration by the Holy Spirit of the individual in the early morning of life.

Third, that Christian Education which prepares one for the duties of life, and produces intelligent, conscientious citizenship.

Fourth, industry, beginning in early youth, that will take the place of the advantages of the city gymnasium; hoe-handle exercises that will make one healthy, industrious, guarding against wastefulness and producing a spirit of economy.

Fifth, the prompt enforcement of law, so that those who are criminally inclined will be deterred, realizing that if they do violate the law they will be promptly and severely punished. Leaving out the items mentioned above, or any one of them, we break the strong, golden chain that would bind our civilization together for the very best there is for the times in which we are living, and the future history of our country. I am hoping this booklet will have a wide circulation and thoughtful reading.

Respectfully,
H. C. MORRISON.

CONTENTS

CHAPTER I.

THE HICKORY LIMB

A new-born babe is one of the most helpless, dependable creatures in the world and, at the same time, most interesting and lovable. It would be a cold, hard heart that would not respond to the plaintive wail of a baby. Left to itself, a babe would soon die; it requires most watchful care.

One of the first things a babe responds to is its sense of taste. For some time it is governed almost entirely by the tip of its tongue, rather than by its intelligence or conscience. So soon as it gets sufficient strength to exercise its members we notice that, when its elbow bends, its mouth flies open. It will eat stone coal as readily as it would angels' food, or drink a deadly poison as quickly as it would drink nutritious milk.

So completely is a babe or child controlled by taste that it is constantly seeking for the pleasure it derives from tasting things; as a result, when its mother's back is turned it slips its hand quickly, though slyly, into a convenient sugar-bowl. Young children are largely controlled by appetite and taste. In many large congregations I have asked that all men who did not steal sugar when small boys to stand up; I have not found one who could stand on that test. This sugar proposition covers a larger variety of appealing articles of food.

This petty pilfering is usually confined for a while to the tid-bits that can be slyly appropriated about one's home. If this inclination is not properly restrained, it frequently falls into a habit that extends its field of operation, and soon the little thief is pilfering a neighbor's apple orchard and melon patch; thus many a criminal record has been begun which has led to hold-ups, bank robberies, murders and the gallows or electric chair.

It is an interesting but sad fact that, in the criminal wave that has for a decade and more been sweeping over this nation, a very large per cent of those guilty of violation of law are in their teens or early twenties. These crimes are by no means limited to minor

offences, but are of a character former-
ly committed by hardened criminals. A
community is often shocked by the murder of father or mother, sometimes both
parents, by a son or daughter under
twenty years of age, for no other rea-
son than that the parent refused to
gratify some whim, or oppose some im-
proper conduct on the part of their off-
spring who, in a frenzy of hatred, without hesitation, shoots down its parents.

If you will make inquiry of grocery
merchants in cities, towns and villages,
they will tell you that many children
have to be watched closely, or they will
take advantage when a clerk's back is
turned, to snatch fruit or sweetmeats,
and get away with anything they can
lay their hands on; and this pilfering is
not confined to children of the slums, or
of the very poor. A brilliant writer, in
a recent issue of *The Forum*, one of our
best monthly publications, tells us of a
druggist who informed him that after
basketball games, when the youngsters
of the school were turned loose, he closed
his store rather than suffer the break-

age and theft that poured in upon him.

It is well understood that a child left to its natural inclination, without proper direction, restraint and correction by older persons, to have its will and way, will most certainly become a disturbing member of society. One of the great needs of the times is a revival of family government, where children are controlled and guided by the brains, the heart, and the experience of their parents, until they have developed intelligence and character of their own.

That teaching of scripture has been very largely ignored which says, "Train up a child in the way it should go, and when he is old he will not depart from it." Solomon further says, "Withhold not correction from the child, for if thou beatest him with the rod he shall not die. Thou shalt beat him with the rod and save his soul from hell." Prov. 23:13, 14.

This word *beat* sounds a bit harsh; let's substitute for it *chastise*. The instruction of Solomon is quite in conflict with modern psychiatrists, writers and teachers who contend that any mode of corporal punishment is wrong. Sometime ago in conversation with one of the great preachers of the gospel in this country, he was telling me of how much he owed to his saintly mother, of his early inclinations to waywardness, and how his mother prayed for him and "spanked the meanness out of him."

Wide observation leads me to believe that children who grow up under kind, but strict discipline, sometimes enforced by the slipper, or rod, on a convenient part of the anatomy, not only make better citizens, but feel more respect and affection for their parents than those young people who grow up without restraint and correction.

This writer is confident that the teaching of evolution in the schools—that we came from brute ancestors—has much to do with the beastly conduct of many of our young people. It is quite probable that philosophers, searching after the cause and cure of the vandalism, disobedience and crime among the youth of the land, have entirely failed in their diagnosis. It is likely that a large per cent of this lawlessness comes from lack of intelligent, positive family government and, it may be, that an ounce of hickory limb, properly applied, would be better than ten pounds of a policeman's billy later in life.

We can think of nothing more cruel and reprehensible than an angry parent beating a child unmercifully. One of the worst men I have ever known told me that when he was a lad fifteen years of age his father, who was a very strong man, in a heat of passion at some minor offense, seized a limb and beat him severely. He tried to explain; he begged; he plead for mercy; he fell upon his knees and entreated his father, who paid no attention to his cries, but continued to smite him in a most unmerciful manner. He said he rolled on the ground, foamed at the mouth, cursed his father with the most bitter oaths and turned into a demon. He said, "I ran away from home. I hated my father and I had murder in my heart. I have been a criminal for years. The cruel treatment of my father changed me from a very good sort of boy into a demon. I have lived a life of crime against God and humanity."

Such parents are not fit to have the care and control of children. I know a family where the children grew up under wise but strict discipline; not tyrannical, but insisted upon obedience, guarded the children against falsehood, theft, discourtesy to neighbors and teachers, or imposition upon small children of other families. The rod was frequently used, without excitement or severity, but in such a way that its use was rarely necessary. Out of that family came a great doctor, one of the best dentists in a large city, a college professor, a fine gospel preacher, an excellent and prosperous farmer, who is a blessing to the social and religious life of his community, and two most excellent daughters.

It is impossible to train up a family of children to be honest, truthful, decent, and to make of them sober, intelligent, useful citizens, without intelligent family government that insists upon and has obedience in a way that brings the child to trust in and respect the wisdom and affection of those who have them in care and training.

After a long life and wide observation, I am fully convinced that one of the great needs of our times is a proper application of the *hickory limb*.

CHAPTER II.

THE MOURNER'S BENCH

Some people of the present generation may not understand the little picture on the cover of this booklet, nor the term, "Mourner's Bench." When I was a lad, the term was well understood, especially among Methodists. It was a little bench that sat in front of the pulpit, to which penitent sinners went and kneeled to pray for the forgiveness of their sins and salvation by faith in Christ.

There are many thousands and tens of thousands of souls in Paradise today who found Jesus Christ as a personal Savior at the mourner's bench. It will be well understood that there is no virtue in a bench, by whatever name it may be called, but it was good for the sinner, before the congregation and community, to rise up in open surrender and come forward and kneel at that humble little altar, as a confession of sin before his fellowbeings, throwing him or herself upon the mercy of God.

If the Scriptures teach anything,

15

they teach that human nature is fallen; that the evil effects of sin are as universal as humankind. In order to pardon there must be repentance. Our Lord Christ has said positively, and with repetition that, "Ye must be born again." This statement of Jesus Christ is applicable, not to humanity in the mass, but to each individual. The religion of Christ is personal. God in some things may deal with the multitude, but when it comes to the forgiveness of sins, and that strange and blessed transaction, which our Lord called the *new birth*, it is just as personal as a physical birth.

Men are not physically born in the mass, but one by one they come into this world, into a conscious state of existence, and each one grows up as a person, distinct from all other persons. It is just so with reference to repentance. This is not a matter that can be attended to in a great mass of people, a sort of social reform, or uplift; but the individual sinner must repent of his or her sins, must forsake sin, exercise saving faith, and be born of the Spirit. He must pass from spiritual death to spiritual life.

One of the great needs of the times is the mourner's bench, well crowded with individuals seeking forgiveness, and that new life which comes from Christ in the gracious operation of the Holy Spirit which makes each individual a new creature and, whereas that individual once loved sin and committed it with eagerness and pleasure, it now hates sin, guards against it, watches and prays for deliverance from temptation, and delights in the law of the Lord, keeps the commandments, and communes with the Holy Spirit.

There has been, it appears, a sort of race between the various denominations of this country for members, a boasting of the large number that this or that church enrolls. The emphasis has been laid more upon *quantity* than *quality*, and it is evident that the mourner's bench has been sadly avoided and forsaken, and multitudes of people without any profound conviction for sin, without the regenerating power of the Holy

Spirit, have come into our churches and continued to live quite like they did before making a profession, receiving baptism without a new heart or any intention or effort to live separate from the worldly multitude about them, and walk in humble, glad obedience to the teachings of our Lord and Saviour.

It is plain to see the great numbers of church members who pay no heed to that saying of Christ in which he gives us to understand that if we would become his disciples we must deny ourselves, take up our cross, and follow him. When the church receives large numbers of people without the regenerating grace of God, they have the same unchanged sinful natures, the same loves and the same hatreds. They look for their pleasures, amusements and pastimes to the same sources from which they derived them before their profession, baptism, and entering into the church. Such large numbers of people of this character have been received into our churches that worldliness abounds; all sorts of entertainments and pastimes, which cannot possibly be a means of grace, are introduced into the church. Devout people are grieved, and sinners on the outside are amused and disgusted.

The reader will readily understand I am not making a plea for the little bench of other days, called the "mourner's bench;" I am simply using it as a symbol of repentance, of a place of prayer, of earnest seeking of the soul's salvation by faith in our crucified and risen Christ.

One thing is sure: A worldly church cannot bring a lost world to Christ. And it is well understood by thoughtful people everywhere, within the church and on the outside, that there is a great slump in spiritual life which has resulted in the lowering of moral standards, and is having a fearful effect on individuals, the home, and the entire life of the nation.

The standards that have been set up in preaching and teaching in this great country of ours have been too low. We are in need of the ministry of such men as Charles Finney who, with the sword of the Spirit, searched the lives and hearts of the people and brought great numbers of church members to realize their lost condition, repent of their sins, and seek the peace and rest for their souls which can be found only at the foot of the cross, trusting in the Christ who died thereon for our redemption.

Somewhere for each individual who would be saved, there must be a place of repentance, of sorrow for sin, of deep grief and mourning, because of a profound sense of having sinned against a compassionate, patient and merciful God. One of the greatest needs of this nation is a tidal wave of conviction for sin, a godly sorrowing and turning away from wickedness. Somewhere between the present state of those who are in rebellion and sin against God, and a state of salvation, there must be a time and place of godly sorrow, acceptance of Christ as an only Savior, and a blessed consciousness that sins are forgiven.

If we have a revival that will save this nation, bring back the sacredness of the home and the marriage vow, replace the Bible, and make the house of God a place of communion with the blessed Trinity, that revival must begin within the church. The ministry must sound loud, long, and insistently the teaching of our Lord Jesus Christ, "Except a man be born again, he cannot see the kingdom of God."

It was an unfortunate hour in the history of Methodism when Decision Day was substituted for the annual revival in Methodist churches. In the salvation of the individual, there must be a *decision*, a forsaking of sin, a seeking of Christ and tarrying in prayer for assurance of pardon, which will always be witnessed by the Holy Spirit to those who forsake all sin and trust in Christ for forgiveness.

Children can be converted—and by this word I mean regenerated—very young. It is just as easy to lead them to Christ as it is to teach them the Catechism, which is quite proper, but it cannot take the place of the work of the Holy Spirit, making the child, in Christ, a new creature. I well remember when a small child, I had a deep sense of my need of a Saviour, and I am confident I could have been genuinely saved, had I have had proper instruction, when I was six years of age.

There are those who teach that a child does not need a sense of sin, to repent, to pray at an altar, to seek the Lord, as older persons do, and to have a definite experience of forgiveness and the peace which that brings to the soul. Such teaching is not only wrong, but dangerous, and has become common, and has defrauded a vast number of our church members out of the gracious experience of regeneration.

It should be remembered that this matter of making the individual a new creature in Christ, is wrought by the Holy Spirit, and one of his most gracious works is revealing to the individual, young or old, the fact that that individual is lost in sin, and must experience a change of heart, which will mean a change of the entire attitude, a definite change of life; a child can have a very profound sense of its lostness and its need of a Saviour; and it can easily be led, with proper instruction, to trust in Jesus, and experience a sense of forgiveness and love that it can carry on the voyage of life, both as sail and anchor. There is nothing finer and more helpful in the hour of temptation, than a clear and gracious memory of the time and place where one met with God in the salvation of the soul.

In the fifty-eight years of my ministry I have traveled among the churches as extensively as any other living man, in evangelistic work. I have preached in our greatest city churches, in towns, county seats, villages, country churches, isolated communities, tents, brush arbors, and in this work I have come in close personal contact with thousands of church members; I find numbers of church members who were brought into the church on Decision Day who have never been born of the Spirit, and have no assurance of sins forgiven. They are not hypocrites, but did what they were told to do; but when they read in the Scriptures of the peace and joy, the witness of the Spirit, and those gracious experiences, they know nothing, whatever, of them by experience.

These unfortunate people become the easy victims of modernistic teachers who, in time, may destroy their faith in every essential truth of the Bible; others, in the hungering of their hearts, can be drawn away to the Christian Scientists, Unity, and other false philosophies which promise them peace, which their Decision Day religion fails to bring them. To undertake to prove the Bible Wesleyan doctrine of entire sanctification to these unregenerated people, is like casting pearls before swine. Having not received the first work of grace, the new birth, they are unprepared to receive the second work of grace, the crucifixion of the carnal nature.

One of the greatest needs of our time is a revival within the church; the regeneration of vast numbers of people who have been brought into the church on Decision Day and Easter occasions, and often at the ordinary Sunday services, without any experience of the gracious work of the Holy Spirit, making them the children of God.

CHAPTER III.

The open book on the cover of this pamphlet stands for education. It is a tragedy that any human being should be shut up in the prison house of illiteracy and ignorance. One of the highest duties of the family, church and state is that of the education of the youth of the land.

Among the many enterprises that are being set on foot in this time of experiments, one could wish that there was a widespread and determined effort to bring the benefits of the rudiments of a common school education to every person under our beautiful flag. Illiteracy ought not to exist in a country like ours. By some means sufficient training ought to be brought to every person, not only the young but to older people who have had no educational advantages, so they could at least read and write.

How unfortunate the blind who cannot see the glories of our physical world and the beauties with which they are surrounded in sunrise and sunset, the

26

towering mountains, the great trees,
the beautiful shrubs, the fresh flowers,
the birds with their colored plumage.
One always grieves to look upon a person who is blind and walking in darkness without the hope or possibility of
looking out upon our world with its
changing panorama of constant attrac-
tion, beauty and wonder.

How unfortunate that person with
blind mentality, who has no power to
read, who knows nothing of the world's
literature, who cannot scan the daily
news, or turn with delight the pages of
history, or read the heart throbs of the
poets who have written down the soul's
deepest emotions and highest aspirations; for a human being to go groping
about in ignorance of all the vast re-
sources of literature, science, philoso-
phy, fiction, travel, story, with none of
the enjoyment or consolations of searching the Scriptures; of the delightful
pastime of reading the history of one's
native land, of perusing the pages
which contain the best thought of the
world's greatest thinkers, or amusing

one's self with the interesting stories which carry such charm as to make one forget their cares. Sad indeed are those who cannot read the Holy Scriptures, inform themselves of the dealings of God with men, ponder the wisdom of the Proverbs, tune their hearts to the songs of David, follow the teachings of Christ, or journey with St. Paul in his evangelistic tours, or stand amazed at the lifting of the curtains of the future in Revelation.

One of the highest duties of parents is to look after the early education of their children, to teach them to study the proper books, to place before them not only the textbooks of the schools but to furnish them with reading that will charm and instruct them, that will not only develop their intellect but mold, strengthen, and build good character. No child, white or black, red or yellow, in this nation, or its possessions, should go without the rudiments of an education. They should at least be taught to good books, reading matter of a character to create a desire for learning and that will promote clean moral thinking, and have a tendency to produce high ideals and build good citizenship.

May I suggest to any reader of this booklet that while you may not be able to open the eyes of the blind, in order that they may see the beauties of nature, you may be able to help some person who has not had the advantages of an education; you may open mental eyes that will bring enlargement of life, the development of intellectual capacity, and create within some unfortunate person, by your assistance, an intellectual hunger that might lead on to greatness, that will at least add wonderfully to a life that otherwise would be drab, dull, uninteresting, and largely unprofitable.

The great English writer, Blair, in one of his essays has a sentence that reads thus: "If in springtime there be no buds, in summer there will be no beauty, and in autumn there will be no fruit. If youth is barren of improvement, manhood will be contemptible, and old age will be miserable."

How unfortunate are those who have no opportunity for education and mental culture, and how reprehensible those who have opportunity for education, who could walk the paths of science, roam the wide field of literature, enjoy the story and songs of human history, and yet refuse, or fail to improve their opportunity and seek out of the best of the literature of the past that which will enlarge their capacities for usefulness and happiness, enabling them to make the most generous contribution to the advancement of human happiness, civilization and progress of mankind.

I cannot lay too much emphasis upon the importance of religious education. The young mind is hungry for information, hence the many questions of the little folk about our feet and knees. They want to know; the young mind is retentive; even in our old age, we find what we learned as children, remains permanently with us. Then, how important the fundamental truths of Christianity, like beautiful filling, be woven into the warp of the education of the young, so that, from their childhood, they have a consciousness of the Divine Being, his presence, his providential care, his guiding wisdom and compassionate love. Into the early life, and throughout the mental training of children and young people, there should be so deeply ingrafted a profound reverence for God, and a belief in his revealed truth, that it will grow into their beings and produce the fruits of righteousness and good citizenship. Men and women who fear God and keep his commandments can safely guide the affairs of Church and State, which will always mean the sacredness of the home, the guarded liberties of the people, and the safe and constant development of our American civilization.

Unfortunately, much of our education today is not only without religious emphasis, but is decidedly *anti*-religious. It is a lamentable fact that many teachers in our common schools, colleges and universities are atheistic. The trend of their thought and teaching faces toward the "far country" of unbelief.

and, worse still, immorality. It is most unfortunate, indeed, it is reprehensible, that the State should employ and pay infidels to lead the youth of the land into the wide wilderness of all of those false philosophies that deny the existence of God, the divine revelation from him as written in the Holy Scriptures, and our obligation of reverence and obedience to God, justice and helpfulness toward our fellowbeings.

How fortunate those children who, in their home training, are so rooted and grounded in religious truth, that in after years it is impossible to tear them away from their spiritual moorings, destroy their faith, break down their Christian character and lead them into the "far country," from which few prodigals return, and many finally starve about the swine-pens of their own lusts and sin.

CHAPTER IV

EMPLOYMENT.

One of the most sacred trusts of any country is its child life. The youth of today is the citizenship of tomorrow. Directly, the children at our fireside and in our schools will govern and control the destiny of the nation.

Our best citizens do not come from the very wealthy classes where children grow up in luxury and idleness, with little or no responsibility, but with ample time to indulge their appetites and stimulate their more dangerous inclinations; neither do they come from the very poor class where children do not have necessary nutriment, or the comforts and opportunities to encourage and draw out that which is best in them.

Our best citizens come from the vast middle class; those people who, by industry and frugality, are able to live respectably, with many of the common comforts of life, whose children are taught industry and assist their parents cheerfully in those lighter services which they can perform without damage to themselves, physically or men--tally, who become habituated to work, and that economy which most children practice who are taught to earn their own spending money.

Through a long life, much travel and wide observation, I have been impressed with the fact that a vast majority of our most successful and influential men, as lawyers, physicians, preachers, business men, teachers, and that army of respectable people who make up a worthwhile and progressive population, come from the middle class of respectable, industrious people by whom they were taught the important lessons of industry and economy.

Having been a College President for a number of years, and having contact with thousands of young people, I have had opportunity to observe that many of those students who worked to pay part of their expenses through school, developed the best character; they do not neglect their studies, they become self-reliant; while learning how to exercise their mental faculties, they also become accustomed to the exercise of their physical being, and on the whole, such students are better prepared for the battle of life than those who have the advantages of wealth, and do not enjoy the privilege of honest and worthy physical service.

It is quite probable if Abraham Lincoln had been born of wealthy parents, had grown up in a city, attended high school, lived in idleness, attended a dozen dances each semester, and spent a few nights each week in some vaudeville show, we never would have heard of him. He had the advantage of silence, of time for meditation, of hard work, of the careful improvement of whatever leisure came to him in study. His intellectual and moral life rooted itself in toil, longing, aspirations and—behold the man!

King David, one of the greatest men of ancient times, the musician and poet who wrote the Psalms, the hymn book of the Hebrews, grew up in the midst of toil and responsibility. As a lad, he

herded his father's sheep when bears
and lions were plentiful and mutton
hungry; but he had learned the use, under these trying circumstances, of all of
his physical powers, and was one of the
very best rock throwers of his time. He
practiced on lions and bears which he
slew with slingstones until he was
ready to strike down the armed champ-
ion of the Philistines, turn the tide of
battle, and save his nation. He never
could have hurled the stone at Goliath
with such accuracy if he had not grown
up in earnest, cheerful toil protecting
his father's sheep.

I am in full sympathy with Agur's
spirit when he prays, "Remove far from
me vanity and lies: give me neither pov-
erty nor riches; feed me with food convenient for me: lest I be full, and deny
thee, and say, Who is the Lord? Or lest
I be poor, and steal, and take the name
of my God in vain." Prov. 30:8, 9.

Wide observation and considerable
experience among my fellowbeings com-
pel me to believe that the best homes in
which to grow sons and daughters, who

will eventually become leaders of the
people, are the homes of the middle-
class families that live industriously,
frugally and piously, where every member of the family has its task, properly
adjusted to its age and capacity, and
performs the same in happy harmony
with the best interests of a well regulated home.

There is a proposed amendment to
the Constitution of the United States,
should it be ratified by three-fourths
of the states of the Union, Congress will have power to regulate and
prohibit the labor of all children under
the age of eighteen years; in other
words, the Federal Government would
take charge of the child and youth life
of this nation. It would not seem possi-
ble that any state legislature would vote
for such a law, and yet, quite a number of state legislatures have done this
very thing.

One is curious to know where such a
proposition originated. It has a strong
odor of Soviet Russia, and there is no
question in the mind of this writer, but

that it is the effort of the communistic spirit to get hold of and control the young life of this nation. Sometime ago, Miss Frances Perkins, United States Secretary of Labor, discussed this child labor amendment to the Constitution in an issue of *The Forum*, and by the way, she is a strong advocate of this amendment to the Constitution. Parents should make a note of this fact.

The proposed amendment would be to give power "to Congress to limit, control and prohibit the labor of all persons under eighteen years of age." Miss Perkins makes a plea for this amendment, and makes various claims in which she endeavors to camouflage the danger of such legislation. In her discussion she says, "The claim that it, the amendment, was inspired by communists, is most incomprehensible."

The fact is, that in a discussion before the Committee, it was learned that the amendment was drafted by Mrs. Florence Kelley Wischnewetzky. What a name! That's certainly Russia!

What business has a woman with that sort of name undertaking to interfere with our Constitution? It appears also, that she was assisted by Mrs. Julia Lethrop, Grace Abbott and Anna Louis Strong. It turns out that this woman, with the difficult name, beginning Kelley, has been a disciple of Engels, a leading communist of Germany, and she was the editor in Berlin, Germany, of a socialistic paper. It appears that she has been a lobbyist about Washington for socialistic legislation. Miss Strong was once an American press agent for the Moscow Soviets, and editor of the *Moscow News*. Miss Abbott has been fed up on the same sort of pabulum with the other members of this group. With these facts before her, how is it that Miss Perkins will deny communistic influence is seeking to get hold of the young life of this nation?

What sort of family government could we have if children grow up with the understanding that their parents have practically no control over them, and cannot command them to perform any simple task or service about the home. You will never convince this writer that these women do not represent the spirit of Soviet Russia; and it would seem impossible that any group of legislators could be found ignorant enough to be beguiled into voting for any such legislation.

The time has come when this Perkins woman should hear from an intelligent and indignant people all over this nation. Legislators, congressmen and senators should be duly warned against any legislation that would interfere with the practical regulation of the child life of the American home. Children should be protected from the slavery which was once imposed upon many of them in cotton mills and factories, and most states have such legislation.

This chapter is being written in the state of Florida, and I find that this state has certain laws for the protection of children which seem to me to be practical, that safeguard the childhood of the country, and at the same time, do not interfere with proper family government. In the state of Florida, no boy under ten years of age, and no girl under sixteen years of age, can be lawfully employed in selling newspapers in any city of the state of 6,000 population or more. Selling and distributing newspapers is hardly the work of a girl, and certainly not the work of any girl in a considerable city. The reader will note that this law does not prohibit the selling of papers in towns or villages where the child is much safer and better protected than in larger populations.

The law provides that children under twelve years of age are not permitted to work in stores, offices, or in the transmission or sale of merchandise, or the delivery of messages. This protects children from dangers involved and temptations that they may not be old enough to resist. No child under fourteen years of age is permitted to work in mills, factories, workshops, mechanical establishments, laundries, or on the stage of any theater. The reader will remember that children under fourteen

years of age are small and tender and
not fitted for heavy work that would
stultify their physical growth or subject
them to the dangers of machinery of
factories and mills. It is a good law
that forbids young children to act upon
theatrical stages. The law also provides that persons under sixteen years
of age cannot be employed in mills or
factories except by permission given by
the county superintendent of public
schools, after that official has made a
careful and thorough investigation of
all facts involved.

The next prohibition is very excellent. No person under twenty-one years
of age may lawfully be employed in any
pool-room, billiard-room, brewery, sa-
loon or bar-room where intoxicating
liquors are sold. The law also provides
for the safety, comfort and protection
of children coming within the prohibi-
tive age. It occurs to this writer that
these laws are reasonable, equitable,
protective, without any effort to interfere with the common services that can
be rendered by children in the life of
any well regulated family.

It is high time that the people of these United States awake to the dangers that beset us on every hand, from visionaries and dreamers who would legislate laws that would take all of our much beloved freedom away from us, and tie us hand and foot in the exercise of common liberty, personal freedom, and the direction and control of our individual affairs.

Russia, Germany, Italy, and a number of other countries have either willingly, or under compulsion, given up the entire spirit of true democracy and exalted despots, who rule the people with a rod of iron, and having, while they promised freedom, enslaved the masses of the people and do not hesitate to slaughter in cold blood any one who interferes with their despotic control of an enslaved and oppressed people.

The people of this nation ought, en masse, insist upon the maintaining of their personal liberty. Of course, this should be without selfishness and a spirit of co-operation for the best interests of the entire people; but it is not to the best interests of any people that communism thrust in upon us its exaggerated and dictatorial spirit that means the wreckage of all of the best and highest ideals of our American civilization.

Children should, and must be, protected from physical slavery, hard work and heavy burdens that would stultify the development of their bodies, hinder the advantages of education and opportunities for exercise, innocent amusement and healthful play. These are the rights of children, which are sacred and should be secured, if necessary, by the legislation of proper and equitable laws.

The drift is in the direction of extreme and fanatical legislation and usages which are out of harmony with our past history, the teachings of Holy Writ, and all of those things that contribute to the growth and development of the best American life and spirit. "Eternal vigilance is the price of liberty." The good people of this nation must be awake and ready for action, and we do not want men and women with those unpronounceable Russian names, and their coadjutors, to be lobbying around the halls of congress, in the capital of our nation. The proper use of the hoe handle is a means of grace; healthy toil is excellent exercise; it fosters an appetite, assists digestion and is followed by restful sleep, growth and development of all that is best in the building of sturdy, self-reliant American citizenship.

CHAPTER V
THE POLICEMAN'S BILLY

The little picture of the policeman's billy on the cover of this book signifies the enforcement of law. We can have no such thing as a safe and progressive civilization without law for the government, protection and proper adjustment of the economic and social relationships which exist among men.

The true statesman is the man who is able to study, search out and legislate into law the principles of justice and equity which should obtain in a well regulated community, state and nation, composed of intelligent beings. Law, without penalty attached, calling for the punishment of those who disregard or violate law, would be of no benefit to mankind; there must be adequate punishment for those who violate law.

If laws are not enforced and the guilty punished, it becomes a dead letter and the lives and property of the people are at the mercy of those whose greed and viciousness know no law.

46

The disregard of law, of the rights
and liberties of others, and the failure
to arrest and inflict punishment upon
the lawless, brings discord, confusion,
riot, mobs, and the destruction of all
that is worth while for the happiness,
peace and prosperity of a civilized people.   We regret to be compelled to record the fact that the United States has
become, in a large per cent of its population, one of the most lawless nations in
the world.   Crime of every description
is constantly committed in this great
country of ours, and while there is not
adequate punishment, and a large per
cent of our criminals go unwhipped of
justice, yet the money expended in the
work of our courts, the employment of
our officials, the trials and confinement
of our criminal population amount to
hundreds of millions of dollars annual-
ly.

If, by the waving of some magic
wand, crime could be made to disappear, the money now expended in the
prosecution of criminals, and their confinement in prison, would be ample to

provide free hospitals for all of our cities, excellent institutions for care of all of our orphans, pensions to provide amply for all of our aged people who are not in condition to care for themselves, and our land would be blessed with a peace and happiness approaching that gracious state supposed to exist in the Millennium.

What are the causes of the great tidal wave of crime that so constantly rolls over this nation? Petty thieving calls for a lock on every door; hold-ups that make it dangerous to walk the streets of village, town or city after dark; the bold and hazardous robbery of banks; the shooting down of helpless people for a few dollars; sometimes enraged robbers kill their victim because he does not possess the few dollars.

We are not thinking so much now of the dishonest money-getting schemes in high places, the sale of worthless bonds, the various life insurance enterprises that rob the people and leave them without hope of remuneration, the army of bankers in government prisons, the graft that is so characteristic in the administration of office, from the village to the towns and great cities. So much dishonesty and graft have been revealed in high and low places within the past few years, that it has come to pass that, to be an official, with an opportunity for pelf, means to be surpicioned. We have come to a very serious situation in our country, which greatly retards the restoration from the depres sion, and that is, loss of confidence. There has been so much of dishonesty that people have become suspicious of each other.

Nations have come to regard solemn and signed treatise as mere "scraps of paper." Great governments have refused to pay their just debts; the repudiation of sacred obligations has become so common that one is reminded of the statement of the Apostle Paul when he declared that, "In the last days perilous times shall come. For men shall be lovers of their own selves, covetous, boasters, proud, blasphemers, disobedient to parents, unthankful, unholy, without natural affection, trucebreakers, false accusers, incontinent, fierce, despisers of those that are good, traitors, heady, high-minded, lovers of pleasures more than lovers of God; having a form of godliness, but denying the power thereof; from such turn away." 2 Tim. 3:1-5.

Satan has been called the "lawless one." He is the enemy of all good order, peace, harmony, reverence and everything that brings permanent happiness and prosperity to humankind. It seems that he has broken loose with a strange and destructive power in the homes, among the youth, in the schools, the church, the factory, the army, the seats of legislation, the places of business, where men gather for counsel, representing the nations, seeking to avert war and promote peace—everywhere there is a powerful influence of evil that breaks up peace, fosters discontent, selfishness and crime.

ORGANIZED CRIME

One of the causes of crime in this nation is the gathering of vast multitudes of foreign-born people in our large cities, who have lived under oppression, have forsaken homeland and come to this country of opportunity, where they find a chance for riches in loot; they form powerful combinations; they secure the protection of officials with whom they divide the profits of their pilfering. In some of our cities these organizations of robbers are as bold and reckless as the daring pirates who used to sail the seas. In some communities to appear as a witness against a member of these robber gangs, is to invite assassination; the attorney who prosecutes them, and the judge who condemns them, does so at the risk of their lives. I am not unmindful of the fact that many of our most desperate criminals are home products, frequently coming from decent, and apparently, well regulated, law-abiding families.

FAMILY GOVERNMENT

There is no question that much of the crime which is so common and startling, committed by children and youth, is the logical result of a sad lack of family discipline. Many children are allowed to have their own way, almost without any sort of intelligent or positive, parental control. In my wide travels as an evangelist, I have often been entertained in the homes of people supposed to be educated, intelligent and pious, who appeared to have no parental authority over, even small children. The children acted as if they had no respect for their parents, teachers or any one else. They certainly appeared to follow their impulses. Those shallow philosophers who insist that you must never say "don't" to a child, or undertake to control and direct their natural inclinations and impulses, would be delighted to see the utter lack of discipline in a large per cent of our American homes.

For a number of years the writer was president of a college. Directly after school opened we were able to note the students who had grown up without home discipline, or any trace of respectful obedience to their parents. Such students invariably became a source of solicitous concern; and you will find that parents who thought their children were too sweet, beautiful and good to be restrained and disciplined, are almost certain to object to the college officials exercising control or discipline over them.

Children who do not obey their parents will not obey their teachers; students who do not obey their teachers will not obey the police, the judge, or the God of the universe. The spirit of the "lawless one" gets into them and dominates them. Unless some divine power gets hold upon them, they will become criminals, disgrace their families, wind up their career in prison, and spend their eternity in outer darkness. A child can have no more dangerous enemy than an indulgent parent who exercises no intelligent discipline, no rules or laws for the government of the family, and no punishment of any kind to be inflicted because of disobedience.

LAWLESS TOYS

We have in the State of Kentucky, and I suppose every state in the Union, a law forbidding the carrying of concealed weapons. The habit of carrying a deadly weapon that can be used in a moment of excitement and anger, called in the courts, "sudden heat and passion," had led to tens of thousands of killings, and years of sadness and regret behind prison bars. If the law were enforced against the carrying of pistols, crime would be greatly reduced. Millions of toy pistols are sold every year; the imitations are almost perfect; they have with them caps that make quite a report when snapped, and the little fellows armed with these pistols imagine themselves to be desperadoes and charge about in mimic hold-ups and robberies. It seems strange that any parent would buy a toy pistol, and in this way sow the small seeds in the imagination, desires and actions of a child that are likely to prepare the way for the carrying of deadly weapons and the use of them. State legislatures ought to enact laws preventing their manufacture and sale.

THE MOVIES

The moving pictures, as we have them in this country, are breeders of lust and schools of crime. It is difficult to conceive of a group of human beings with such low and selfish greed for gain, that they would, for sheer gain, put before the public, especially the young who are easily impressed and fascinated, the kind of pictures that have flooded this nation with filth for the past decades. They are schools of vice. They dull and deaden the better impulses, arouse and kindle the most dangerous passions that can degrade human beings. It is passing strange that our people permit the existence and display of these pictures so destructive to everything that is good, and the fostering of everything that is evil in human nature. There is much talk, but little action; and these degrading influences are allowed to go forward with their desecration of the home, the marriage relation and the young life of our nation.

THE LIQUOR TRAFFIC

When one comes to think of the liquor traffic he finds ample room and play for righteous indignation. He is forced to the conclusion that money is the god of the godless. It is almost impossible to believe that men and women can become so selfish, such human demons, that they are not only willing, but eager to take advantage of the weakness oi their fellowmen, degrade and destroy them, most miserably, for this life and that which is to come, for money. These liquor demons who manufacture and sell liquor for the destruction of their fellows, can never get enough money. Nothing in all the world has fostered selfishness, greed, crime, misery, degradation, physical death and spiritual ruin, like the liquor traffic.

We assemble the manufacturers of intoxicants, wholesalers, retailers, and lawmakers who, for money, turn the liquor traffice loose upon the people and put them into one great, guilty, godless class of selfish, deluded human beings. We believe that manufacturers, wholesalers, retailers, promoters, voters and the whole outfit, millionaires and paupers, society women and demagogues in political high places, must repent of their evil deeds, or, finally keep company with each other in hell.

The degradation of human beings and lawlessness which has been, is being, and will be, produced by the liquor traffic cannot be estimated by figures or described in human language. Lawmakers and law-enforcers confess that human beings are naturally so weak in virtue and so strong in vice, that laws for the suppression of the liquor traffic cannot be enforced. We are not ready to admit the truthfulness of this statement. We believe laws can be enacted, and officials may be elected, punishment can be so severe, and inflicted so promptly, that the liquor traffic would almost disappear from the land.

Politics have become so corrupt, and politicians so lacking in the high and noble virtues, that the majority of the people of this nation have been led to believe that it is so impossible to enforce prohibitory laws against the manufac-

ture and sale of liquor, that the nation,
the President, Senate, Congress, Gov-
ernors, Legislators, enforcement offi-
cers, and the Church of God must surrender to these evil forces, and make the
liquor traffic legal, and out of the wreck
and ruin of the family, human bodies
and human souls, gather blood money
to support the nation, which means vast
salaries for an army of demagogues.
By this statement we do not mean that
there are no statesmen of honor and integrity, and no officials who are true to
their oath of office; but it looks as if
that same powerful person who offered
Jesus Christ the control of the king-
doms of the earth, if he would fall down
and worship him, had brought the majority of our people to their knees with
his false promises, and largely guides
and controls them in their actions, especially, at the ballot-box.

If we would save this nation, we must
begin with the hickory limb, which, by
no means must stand for cruelty, but it
must mean home discipline; if necessary, the use of the rod to guide the

young along the path of obedience which leads to good character and useful living.

We must recognize the Mourner's Bench, the supreme importance of the office and work of the Holy Spirit in the regeneration of each and every individual who comes to years of responsibility; this gracious work of God secured, the individual, the home and the nation are safe.

We must insist upon Education that considers, not only the body and mind, but the immortal spirit, and is so directed that reverence for God, respect for law, and the principles of integrity are woven into the life of our people in the years in which they secure their education.

We must insist upon toil. Every one should be a willing worker. Useful employment is not only healthy, but a means of development of the spirit of self-support that brings, not only self-respect, but an interest in all others who eat honest bread in the sweat of their brow. A nation of idlers will become a nation of criminals, who will not only violate human, but divine law. There must be a revival of law enforcement. There can, and should be, provided a net that will catch the violator and bring him to the courts of justice. Trials ought to be speedy, and punishment severe. Men should be made to fear to commit crime. No one man should have power to pardon and turn loose criminals upon the public; no one juror should have power to prevent the bringing in of a verdict of "guilty." There ought to be a widespread and general determination to sweep out of existence many of those things which sow the seeds and breed the spirit of lawlessness and crime.

As I approach the sunset of life, looking backward, around me, and forward, I am forced to believe that the five greatest needs of our times are suggested by the little pictures on the front cover of this booklet: The Hickory Limb, The Book, The Mourner's Bench, the Hoe, and the Policeman's Billy.

Let us have wise family discipline,

the regenerating power of God in the hearts of our youth, Christian Education, Industry which provides support and self-respect, and the proper enforcement of law, and our nation is safe, and our people will be a progressive, Christian nation, happy and hopeful in the life that now is, and that which is to come.

Respectfully yours,

H. C. MORRISON.

www.ingramcontent.com/pod-product-compliance
Lightning Source LLC
Chambersburg PA
CBHW020520030426
42337CB00011B/485